DATE DUE

LO QUE HACEN LOS DOCTORES
WHAT DOCTORS DO

What Does a Community Helper Do? Bilingual   Felicia Lowenstein Niven

Words to Know

hospital—A building with doctors, nurses, and equipment to treat sick people.

healthy—Being well, not sick.

germs—Very small living things that can cause one to become sick.

patient—The person being treated.

physician—Another word for doctor.

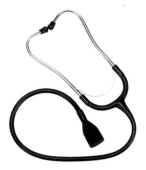

Palabras a conocer

los gérmenes—Organismos muy pequeños que pueden enfermarnos.

el hospital—Un edificio donde hay médicos, enfermeros y equipos para tratar a los enfermos.

el médico—Otra palabra para decir doctor.

el paciente—Persona bajo tratamiento médico.

sano, saludable—Que está bien, que no está enfermo.

Enslow Elementary
an imprint of

Enslow Publishers, Inc.
40 Industrial Road
Box 398
Berkeley Heights, NJ 07922
USA

http://www.enslow.com

Contents/Contenido

The doctor rushed to see his patient.

El doctor se apuró para atender a su paciente.

STAT!

The voice boomed over the hospital speaker.
"Dr. Niven STAT to Room 111."

Dr. Niven was eating lunch. He did not even take another bite. He knew that STAT meant right away. A child was sick. It was his job to help. He moved quickly. He wanted to make it in time.

• •

¡STAT!

La voz retumbó en el altavoz del hospital.
— Dr. Niven, STAT en la habitación 111.

El Dr. Niven estaba almorzando. Ni siquiera tomó otro bocado. El sabía que STAT significaba de inmediato. Un niño estaba enfermo. Su trabajo era ayudarlo. Él fue rápidamente. Quería llegar a tiempo.

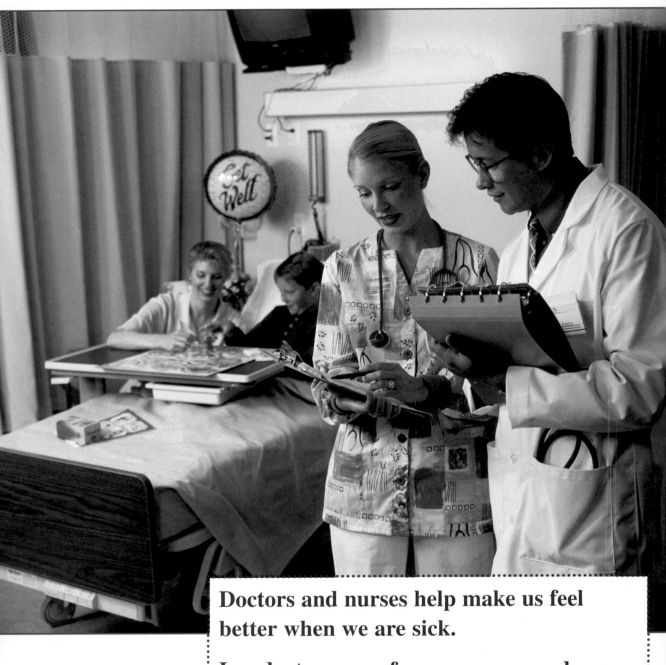

Doctors and nurses help make us feel better when we are sick.

Los doctores y enfermeros nos ayudan a sentirnos mejor cuando estamos enfermos.

Taking Care of Us

Dr. Niven is a **physician**. That is another word for doctor. Doctors take care of us. When we are sick, they help us to feel better. They give us medicine. They are part of the team that keeps us **healthy**.

●●●●●●●●●●●●●●●●●●●●●●●●●●●●●●●●●●●●●

Quiénes nos cuidan

El Dr. Niven es un **médico**. Médico es otra palabra para decir doctor. Los doctores nos cuidan. Cuando estamos enfermos, ellos nos ayudan a sentirnos mejor. Nos dan medicinas. Ellos forman parte del equipo que nos mantiene **saludables**.

Doctors go to school for a long time. They learn about the human body.

Los doctores van a la escuela durante mucho tiempo. Ellos aprenden sobre el cuerpo humano.

Do You Want to be a Doctor?

Do you want to be a doctor? If you do, you have to be good in science and math. You have to like to study. Doctors study for a long time. Becoming a doctor needs more training than almost any other job. It takes about eleven years.

. . . .

¿Quieres ser doctor?

¿Quieres ser un doctor? Si lo deseas, tú tienes que ser bueno en ciencias y matemáticas. A ti tiene que gustarte estudiar. Los doctores estudian durante mucho tiempo. Hacerse doctor requiere más entrenamiento que casi cualquier otro trabajo. Lleva unos once años.

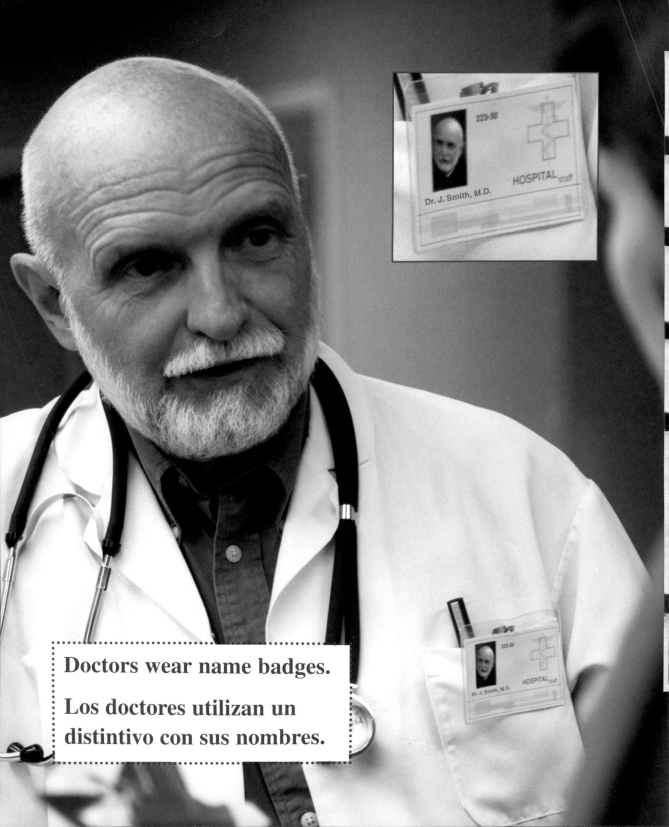

Doctors wear name badges.

Los doctores utilizan un distintivo con sus nombres.

What Does M.D. Mean?

Look at the doctor's name. The two letters, M.D., mean Medical Doctor. That tells you the doctor went to medical school. He worked in a hospital. He passed a test. He knows all the right things to be your doctor.

• •

¿Qué significa M.D.?

Fíjate en el nombre del doctor. Las dos letras, M.D., significan Doctor en Medicina. Esto te indica que el médico se graduó en una escuela de medicina. Él trabajó en un hospital. Aprobó un examen. Él conoce todo lo necesario para ser tu doctor.

eye chart—The doctor uses an eye chart to find out how well you can see.

carta para medir la visión— Los doctores utilizan estas cartas para saber cómo ves.

otoscope—An otoscope helps a doctor see into your ears.

otoscopio— El otoscopio permite al doctor ver dentro de tus oídos.

tongue depressor—The doctor uses this to press your tongue down when looking in your mouth.

depresor lingual—El doctor lo utiliza para presionar la lengua hacia abajo cuando mira dentro de tu boca.

blood pressure cuff—This is used to check how hard your heart is pumping to move blood through your body.

brazalete para medir la presión arterial—Se usa para medir con qué fuerza bombea el corazón para impulsar la sangre a través de tu cuerpo.

stethoscope—A stethoscope lets the doctor listen to your heart and lungs.

estetoscopio— El estetoscopio permite al doctor escuchar tu corazón y tus pulmones.

thermometer—A thermometer will tell the doctor if you have a fever.

termómetro— El termómetro le indica al doctor si tienes fiebre.

reflex hammer—The doctor taps your knee with this to test your reflexes. The doctor wants to see if your leg kicks out on its own.

martillo para reflejos— El doctor golpea tu rodilla con él para examinar tus reflejos. El doctor necesita saber si tu pierna se mueve por sí misma.

A Doctor's Tools

Doctors have special tools. Doctors use these tools to make sure our body is working well. Take a look.

• •

Los instrumentos del doctor

Los doctores tienen instrumentos especiales. Los doctores usan estos instrumentos para asegurarse de que nuestros cuerpos funcionan bien. Observa las fotografías.

These doctors work with people's insides.

Estos doctores se ocupan del interior de las personas.

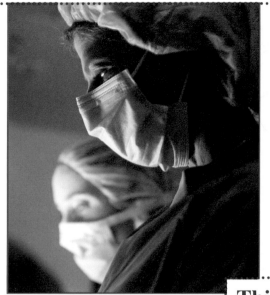

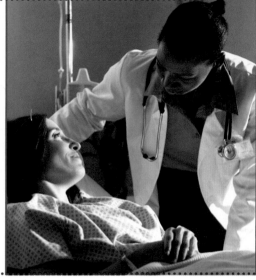

This doctor works in a hospital.

Este doctor trabaja en un hospital.

This doctor works with babies.

Este doctor trabaja con bebés.

Different Jobs

Did you know that not all doctors do the same job? Some work only with children. Some help mothers have babies. Others work with people's insides. There are many jobs. Each doctor has learned his or her special job.

• •

Trabajos diferentes

¿Sabías tú que no todos los doctores hacen el mismo trabajo? Algunos sólo atienden niños. Otros ayudan a las mamás a tener bebés. Otros se ocupan del interior de las personas. Hay muchos trabajos. Cada doctor ha aprendido su trabajo específico.

These doctors make medicines.

Estos doctores hacen medicamentos.

This doctor studies germs.

Este doctor estudia los gérmenes.

This doctor hands out medicine.

Este doctor distribuye medicamentos.

Where Do Doctors Work?

Doctors work in different places, too. Some work in a hospital. Others work in a doctor's office. Still others work for companies that make medicines. Most doctors work with nurses and other health workers.

. . . .

¿Dónde trabajan los doctores?

Los doctores también trabajan en diferentes lugares. Algunos trabajan en hospitales. Otros trabajan en consultorios. Otros trabajan en compañías que hacen medicinas. La mayoría de los doctores trabajan con enfermeros y otros trabajadores de la salud.

This doctor cares for his patient.

Este doctor atiende a su paciente.

When Do Doctors Work?

It seems that a doctor's work is never done. They work long hours. They work in the middle of the night. Even on their days off, doctors may be "on call." That means they have to come in if they are called.

• •

¿Cuándo trabajan los doctores?

Parecería que el trabajo del doctor nunca termina. Ellos trabajan durante muchas horas. También trabajan en el medio de la noche. Aún en sus días libres, muchos doctores deben estar "localizables". Eso significa que ellos tienen que presentarse si se los llama.

One way we can help doctors is by eating the right foods. Doctors make sure we stay healthy.

Una forma de ayudar a los doctores es comer los alimentos adecuados. Los doctores se aseguran de que estemos saludables.

Staying Healthy

Doctors keep us safe and healthy. But they need our help too. We can take care of our bodies. We can get enough sleep. We can eat healthy foods. We visit our doctor when we are feeling fine, too. This way doctors make sure we stay healthy.

• •

Para mantenernos saludables

Los doctores nos mantienen sanos y salvos. Pero ellos también necesitan de nuestra ayuda. Nosotros podemos cuidar nuestros cuerpos. Podemos dormir lo necesario. Nosotros podemos comer alimentos saludables. Nosotros también visitamos a nuestro doctor cuando nos sentimos bien. De este modo los doctores se aseguran de que nos mantengamos saludables.

Wash Up!   ¡A lavarse!

Germs are everywhere. Some germs are good. But most are bad. Germs can make us sick. One way to stay healthy and get rid of germs is to wash our hands.

When Should I Wash Up?

After:
   Using the bathroom
   Blowing or wiping your nose
      with a tissue
   Playing with pets and animals
Before:
   You touch food
   You eat
   You touch your eyes, mouth, or nose

How Do I Wash My Hands?

1. Wet your hands with warm water.

2. Apply some soap.

3. Rub your hands together to make soapy bubbles. Sing your favorite song for 20 seconds.

4. Make sure you wash between your fingers and on the tops and bottoms of your hands. Get your wrists soapy, too!

5. Rinse well.

6. Dry carefully using a cloth towel or paper towel.

Los gérmenes están por todas partes. Algunos gérmenes son buenos. Pero la mayoría son malos. Ellos pueden enfermarnos. Una manera de mantenerse saludable y eliminar los gérmenes es lavándonos las manos.

¿Cuándo debo lavarme las manos?

Después de:
   Ir al baño
   Soplarte o limpiarte la nariz
   Jugar con mascotas y animales
Antes de:
   Tocar alimentos
   Comer
   Tocarte los ojos, la boca o la nariz

¿Cómo me lavo las manos?

1. Mójate las manos con agua tibia.

2. Enjabónatelas.

3. Frótate las manos hasta hacer burbujas de jabón. Canta tu canción preferida durante 20 segundos.

4. Asegúrate que te lavas entre los dedos y las partes de arriba y de abajo de tus manos. ¡Enjabónate también las muñecas!

5. Enjuágate bien.

6. Sécate cuidadosamente utilizando una toalla de tela o papel.

Learn More / Más para aprender

Books / Libros

In English / En inglés

Brill, Marlene Targ. *Doctors*. Minneapolis, Minn.: Lerner Publications, 2005.

Liebman, Dan. *I Want to Be a Doctor*. Toronto, Canada: Firefly Books, 2000.

In Spanish / En español

Miller, Heather. *Médico*. Chicago, Ill.: Heinemann Library, 2003.

Radabaugh, Melinda Beth. *Voy al médico*. Chicago, Ill.: Heinemann Library, 2004.

In English and Spanish / En inglés y español

Gorman, Jacqueline Laks. *Doctor = El médico*. Milwaukee, Wisc.: Weekly Reader Early Learning Library, 2002.

Internet Addresses / Direcciones de Internet

In English / En inglés

KidsHealth for Kids
<http://www.kidshealth.org/kid>
Learn more about staying healthy.

In English and Spanish / En inglés y español

Arthur's Guide to Children's Hospital Boston
<http://www.childrenshospital.org/arthur>
Find out what a doctor's visit is like at this site.

Index

Índice

• •

Note to Teachers and Parents: The *What Does a Community Helper Do?* series supports curriculum standards for K–4 learning about community services and helpers. The Words to Know section introduces subject-specific vocabulary. Early readers may require help with these new words.

Series Literacy Consultant:
Allan A. De Fina, Ph.D.
Past President of the New Jersey Reading Association
Professor, Department of Literacy Education
New Jersey City University

• •

Enslow Elementary, an imprint of Enslow Publishers, Inc.

Enslow Elementary® is a registered trademark of Enslow Publishers, Inc.

Copyright © 2008 by Enslow Publishers, Inc.

Bilingual edition copyright 2008 by Enslow Publishers, Inc.
Originally published in English under the title *What Does a Doctor Do?*
© 2005 by Enslow Publishers, Inc. Bilingual edition translated by Eloísa X. Le Riverend, edited by Susana C. Schultz, of Strictly Spanish, LLC.

All rights reserved.

No part of this book may be reproduced by any means without the written permission of the publisher.

Library of Congress Cataloging-in-Publication Data

Niven, Felicia Lowenstein.
   [What does a doctor do? Spanish & English]
   Lo que hacen los doctores = What doctors do / Felicia Lowenstein.
      p. cm. — (What does a community helper do? bilingual)
   Includes bibliographical references.
   ISBN-13: 978-0-7660-2824-1
   ISBN-10: 0-7660-2824-0
   1. Physicians—Juvenile literature. I. Title.
   R690.L6718 2007
   610.69'5—dc22
                    2006019230

Printed in the United States of America

10 9 8 7 6 5 4 3 2 1

To Our Readers:
We have done our best to make sure all Internet Addresses in this book were active and appropriate when we went to press. However, the author and the publisher have no control over and assume no liability for the material available on those Internet sites or on other Web sites they may link to. Any comments or suggestions can be sent by e-mail to comments@enslow.com or to the address on the back cover.

Illustration Credits: Hemera Technologies, Inc. 1997–2000, pp. 2, 12 (thermometer, otoscope, tongue depressors), 22; © JupiterImages, pp. 1, 4, 6, 8, 12 (stethoscope, eye chart, reflex hammer, blood pressure cuff), 16 (top right and bottom right), 20 (all); RubberBall Productions, pp. 10, 12 (center), 14 (all), 16 (left), 18.

Cover Illustration: © JupiterImages (bottom); top (left to right) © 2004 JupiterImages, RubberBall Productions, © 2004 JupiterImages, © 2004 JupiterImages.